This book is to be returned on or before
the last date stamped below

QCA SCIENCE

119114

D0186537

NORFOLK LIBRARY
AND INFORMATION SERVICE

NORFOLK ITEM

30129 0397 0997 8

R...es

A & C BLACK • LONDON

Reptiles

contents

NORFOLK
LIBRARIES & INFORMATION SERVICE

947150	
PETERS	01-May-03
JF	£15.99

© Blake Publishing Pty Ltd 2002
Additional Material © A & C Black Publishers Ltd 2003

First published 2002 in Australia by Blake Education Pty Ltd

This edition published 2003 in the United Kingdom by
A&C Black Publishers Ltd, 37 Soho Square, London W1D 3QZ
www.acblack.com

Published by permission of Blake Publishing Pty Ltd, Glebe NSW, Australia.
All rights reserved. No part of this publication may be reproduced in any
form or by any means – graphic, electronic or mechanical, including
photocopying, recording, taping or information storage and retrieval systems
– without the prior written permission of the publishers.

ISBN 0-7136-6603-X

A CIP record for this book is available from the British Library.

Written by Paul McEvoy
Science Consultant: Ros Sadlier, Division of Vertebrate Zoology (Reptiles),
Australian Museum
Design and layout by The Modern Art Production Group
Photos by Photodisc, Stockbyte, John Foxx, Corbis, Imagin,
Artville and Corel

UK Series Consultant: Julie Garnett

Printed in Hong Kong by Wing King Tong Co Ltd

A & C Black uses paper produced with elemental chlorine-free pulp,
harvested from managed sustainable forests.

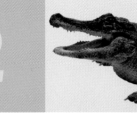

Reptiles are cold-blooded animals with a backbone and scales.

All reptiles are **cold-blooded** animals. This means they need heat from outside their bodies. They use the heat from the sun to warm their bodies.

All reptiles have scales to protect their bodies. The scales make a thick, tough skin.

Reptiles live in warm or hot places. Some reptiles live in the desert. Some reptiles live in the sea.

Most reptiles lay eggs. The eggs have leathery shells. Reptiles lay their eggs on land. The shells protect the baby reptiles while they grow.

4

SMALLEST!

The smallest reptile is a British Virgin Island gecko. It is only 1·7 centimetres long.

Animal	Number of species
reptiles	6 560

The basilisk lizard can run on water to escape from its predators.

Types of Reptiles

There are many different types of reptiles. There are more than 6 000 species of reptiles.

Lizards, crocodiles, snakes and turtles are reptiles. They are cold-blooded animals with a **backbone** and scales. They all need the sun's heat to warm their bodies.

Reptiles live in many different **habitats**. Crocodiles and alligators live in swamps and rivers in warm **climates**.

Reptiles can live in the desert. Some lizards and snakes live in the desert.

Some reptiles live in the sea. Turtles can live in the sea.

Some reptiles live in people's gardens. Lizards can live in gardens.

A frill-necked lizard shows its frills.

Turtles see well under water.

Snakes use their belly scales to help them move.

7

Lizards

Lizards are reptiles. They are cold-blooded animals with a backbone and scales.

Most lizards have four legs and a long tail. Their bodies are covered in scales. Some scales are sharp and spiky. Some scales are bright and colourful.

Lizards live in warm parts of the world. They need the heat from the sun to warm them up. Some lizards can live in hot deserts. Others live in tropical rainforests.

Lizards eat insects, small animals and plants. They can move quickly to catch their food. Many lizards have sharp claws for digging, climbing and catching food.

Galapagos iguanas have colourful scales.

Lizards need heat from the sun.

Lizards are the largest group of reptiles.

GO FACTS

VENOMOUS!

The gila monster and the Mexican beaded lizard are the only **venomous** lizards.

Animal	Number of species
lizards	3 750

A Lizard's Day

How does a lizard spend the day?

1 **Early Morning** At sunrise a lizard moves slowly. It warms itself in the sun before going hunting.

2 **Late Morning** The warm lizard can move quickly. Lizards hunt and catch insects and small animals.

3 **Afternoon** After feeding, the lizard rests in the sun to **digest** its food.

4 **Night** At night the lizard finds a safe place to sleep. During the night the lizard's body cools down. In the morning the lizard can only move slowly.

10

Crocodiles and Alligators

Crocodiles and alligators are reptiles. They are cold-blooded animals with a backbone and scales.

Crocodiles and alligators have four short legs and a long tail. They have long bodies covered in rough scales. They can hide under water and breathe through their noses. Their long tails help them to swim.

Crocodiles and alligators live in warm or hot climates. They need heat from the sun to warm them up. All alligators and crocodiles live near water.

Crocodiles and alligators eat fish and other animals. Their sharp teeth and strong jaws help them to catch their food.

LARGEST!

Crocodiles are the largest reptiles.

Reptile	Number of species
crocodiles	22

Baby crocodiles look like their parents.

An alligator hides low in the water to hunt.

Crocodiles can move quickly to catch food.

13

Life Cycle of a Crocodile

How a crocodile grows from an egg to an adult.

1 A crocodile lays its eggs in a nest under the ground.

2 The mother crocodile protects the eggs until they hatch.

3 The baby crocodiles hatch out of their eggs. The baby crocodiles look just like their parents, only smaller.

4 Baby crocodiles eat insects, frogs and small fish. As the crocodiles grow bigger, they grow new scales.

Snakes

Snakes are reptiles without legs. Like other reptiles, they have a backbone and scales.

Snakes have long, slim bodies covered by scales. Snakes have no legs, but they can move quickly over the ground by wriggling from side to side. Some snakes can climb trees, and others can swim.

Snakes eat small animals. They move very quickly to catch their food. Some snakes, such as pythons, kill by crushing.

Venomous snakes have long, sharp teeth called **fangs**. The fangs are hollow with a hole at the tip. Snakes with fangs kill small animals by injecting them with **venom**.

16

Green tree pythons live in trees.

This snake is smelling the air with its forked tongue.

This emerald tree boa lives in the Amazon rainforest.

GO FACTS

HEAVIEST!

An anaconda can weigh as much as three adults.

Animal	Number of species
snakes	2 400

Poisonous Snakes

How a snake hunts for food.

Some snakes kill using poisonous venom. They have sharp teeth called fangs. When the snake bites, its fangs inject venom into the animal.

1 At sunrise a snake moves slowly out of its hole and into the sun.

2 Snakes have a very good sense of smell. The snake smells the air using its forked tongue.

collecting venom

3 A mouse comes near, looking for food. The snake moves quickly. Its fangs inject venom into the mouse.

4 The mouse dies. The snake swallows the whole mouse.

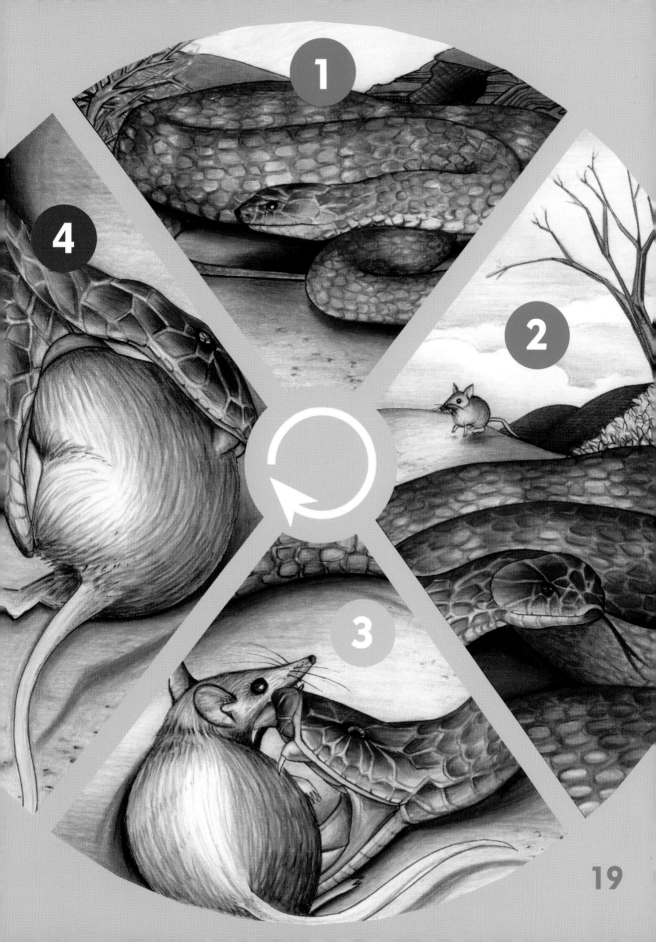

Turtles

Turtles are reptiles. They are cold-blooded animals with a backbone, scales and a hard shell.

Turtles have a hard shell. This hard shell protects them from **predators**. Scales and skin cover the rest of the turtle's body. The scales are smooth.

Most turtles live in ponds and rivers. They feed on insects, small animals such as frogs, and plants. Some turtles live on land.

Some turtles live in the sea. Their feet are shaped like flippers that are good for swimming. Sea turtles come out of the water to lay their eggs in the sand. They eat fish and plants.

A sea turtle must swim to the surface to breathe.

Turtles move slowly on land.

Sea turtles spend most of their time in the ocean.

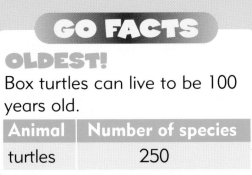

GO FACTS

OLDEST!

Box turtles can live to be 100 years old.

Animal	Number of species
turtles	250

What Reptiles Eat

	Insects	Fish	Plants	Small animals
lizard	✓		✓	✓
crocodile		✓		✓
snake	✓	✓		✓
turtle	✓	✓	✓	✓

 Glossary

backbone	the spine
climate	place with particular weather
cold-blooded	having blood that warms and cools with the surroundings
digest	to break down food so it can be used by the body
fangs	the sharp, hollow teeth of snakes
habitat	the place where an animal or plant lives
predator	an animal that hunts and eats other animals
species	a type or kind of living thing
venom	the poison used by some animals to kill prey
venomous	poisonous

23

Index